MW00975496

EYE OPENERS

Landmarks

BLACKBIRCH®
PRESS

San Diego • Detroit • New York • San Francisco • Cleveland
New Haven, Conn. • Waterville, Maine • London • Munich

LIBRARY OF CONGRESS CATALOGING-IN-PUBLICATION DATA

Nathan, Emma.
  Landmarks / by Emma Nathan.
    p. cm. — (Eyeopeners series)
Summary: Introduces natural and man-made landmarks from different parts of the
world, including the pyramids of Egypt and Ayers Rock in Australia.
Includes bibliographical references and index.
  ISBN 1-41030-028-5 (hardback : alk. paper)
1. Historic buildings—Juvenile literature. 2. Historic sites—Juvenile literature.
3. Monuments—Juvenile literature. 4. History—Miscellanea—Juvenile literature. 5.
World history—Juvenile literature. [1. Historic buildings. 2. Historic sites. 3. Monuments.
4. History—Miscellanea.] I. Title.

D21.3 .N377 2003
909—dc21   2002012465

Printed in United States
10 9 8 7 6 5 4 3 2 1

TABLE
OF
CONTENTS

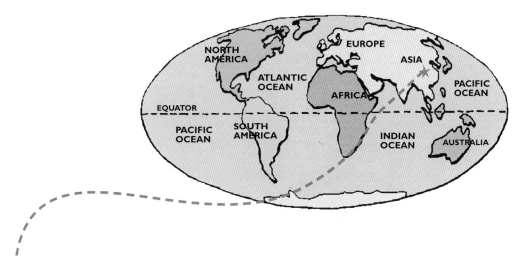

CHINA (CHY-nuh)

China is on the continent of Asia.

The Great Wall of China was built more than 1,300 years ago.

It was built to keep enemies out of China.

The Great Wall is more than 4,000 miles long.

The Great Wall is so big that astronauts can see it from space.

◀ **The Great Wall of China**

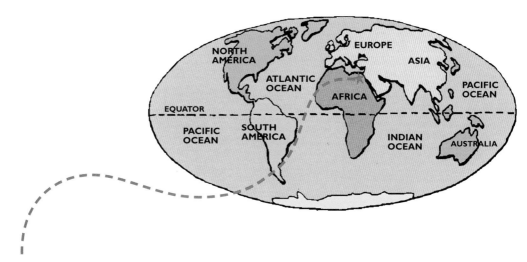

EGYPT (EE-jipt)

Egypt is on the continent of Africa.

People were living in Egypt thousands of years ago.

Ancient Egyptians built large stone pyramids.

The largest pyramid in Egypt is the Great Pyramid at Giza.

The Great Pyramid is 454 feet high.

◀ **Pyramids of Giza**

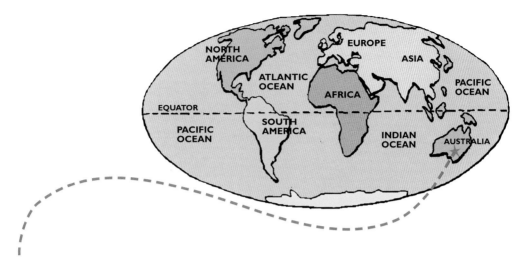

AUSTRALIA (OSS-tray-lee-ah)

Australia is a continent all its own.

Australia's most famous natural landmark is Ayers Rock.

Ayers Rock is a giant red rock that sits on a big flat plain.

Ayers Rock is the world's largest rock.

Ayers Rock is more than 2 miles long and 1.5 miles wide. It is more than 1,000 feet high.

◀ **Ayers Rock**

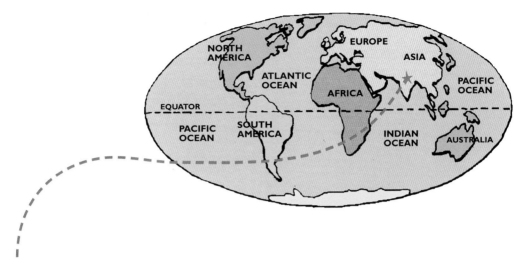

INDIA (IN-dee-ya)

India is on the continent of Asia.

The most famous landmark in India is the Taj Mahal (toj ma-HALL).

The Taj Mahal is a huge building made of white marble.

The Taj Mahal took workers 22 years to build.

A king in India had the Taj Mahal built as a special place to bury his wife.

◄ The Taj Mahal

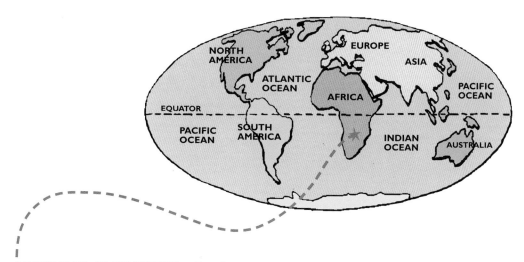

ZIMBABWE (zim-BAH-boo-ay)

Zimbabwe is on the continent of Africa.

Zimbabwe is in southern Africa.

Victoria Falls is a famous waterfall on the northern border of Zimbabwe.

Victoria Falls is more than 350 feet high.

The waterfall is more than 1 mile long.

◀ **Victoria Falls**

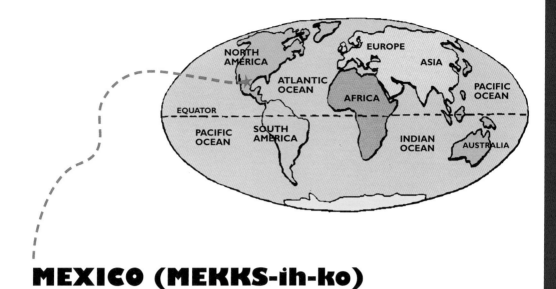

MEXICO (MEKKS-ih-ko)

Mexico is on the continent of North America.

Ancient people in Mexico built large temples out of stone.

The Aztecs were ancient people who built stone temples that looked like pyramids.

The Aztecs built their most famous temple in 1375.

They believed this temple was at the center of the universe.

◀ **Aztec pyramid**

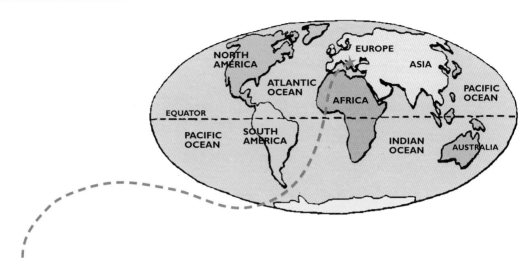

ITALY (IH-tul-ee)

Italy is on the continent of Europe.

2,000 years ago, Italy had the largest empire in the world.

The center of the empire was the city of Rome.

Romans built a huge coliseum in Rome as an entertainment center.

The Coliseum had 80 entrances and could hold 50,000 people.

◀ The Coliseum in Rome

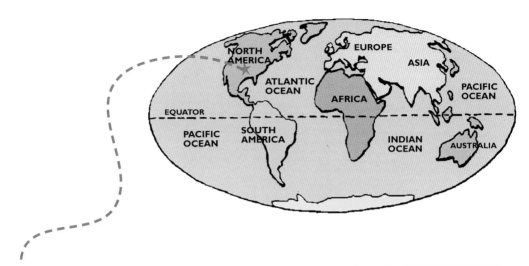

UNITED STATES (yu-nye-ted STAYTS)

The United States is on the continent of North America.

The Statue of Liberty is one of the most famous symbols of American freedom.

The Statue of Liberty stands in New York Harbor. It is 151 feet tall.

France gave the Statue of Liberty to the United States in 1886.

◀ **The Statue of Liberty**

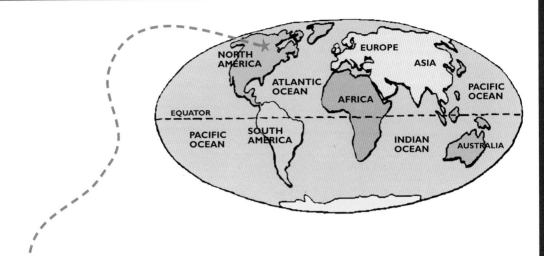

CANADA (CAN-a-duh)

Canada is part of the continent of North America.

Canada's biggest city is Toronto.

The most famous landmark in Toronto is the CN Tower.

The CN Tower is the world's tallest tower. It is 1,815 feet high.

People can ride an elevator to the top and see for miles in every direction.

◀ **The CN Tower**

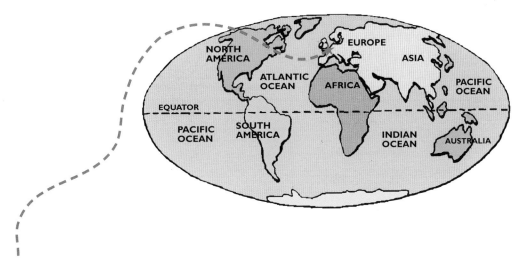

FRANCE (frants)

France is on the continent of Europe.

The most famous landmark in France is the Eiffel Tower.

The Eiffel Tower is in France's capital city of Paris.

The man who designed the tower had worked on the Statue of Liberty.

Visitors have to climb 1,665 steps to get to the top of the Eiffel Tower.

◀ **The Eiffel Tower**

Index

For More Information

Websites

Ayers Rock website
http://www.crystalinks.com/ayersrock.html

The Coliseum
http://www.eliki.com/ancient/civilizations/roman/

The Great Wall of China
http://www.discovery.com/stories/history/greatwall/greatwall.html

The official CN Tower website
http://www.cntower.ca/

The official Eiffel Tower website
http://www.tour-eiffel.fr/teiffel/uk/

The official Statue of Liberty website
http://www.nps.gov/stli/

Victoria Falls National Park website
http://www.wcmc.org.uk/protected_areas/data/wh/victoria.html

Books

Cooper, Jason. *American Landmarks: Discovery Library.* Vero Beach, FL: Rourke Publishing Group, 1999.

Deady, Kathleen. *The Statue of Liberty.* Mankato, MN: Bridgestone Books, 2002.

National Landmarks. Mankato, MN: Bridgestone Books, 2002.